YANNI

SELECTIONS FROM
"IF I COULD TELL YOU" AND "TRIBUTE"

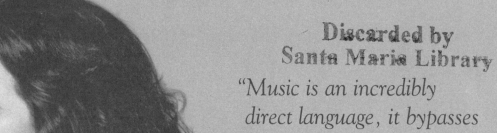
Discarded by
Santa Maria Library

"Music is an incredibly
direct language, it bypasses
logic and speaks directly
to your soul."
— Yanni

"There is no end to
creativity, not as long as
you take the time to live."
— Yanni

Photography by Lynn Goldsmith

ISBN 0-634-02337-3

HAL•LEONARD®
CORPORATION
7777 W. BLUEMOUND RD. P.O. BOX 13819 MILWAUKEE, WI 53213

www.yanni.com

Visit Hal Leonard Online at
www.halleonard.com

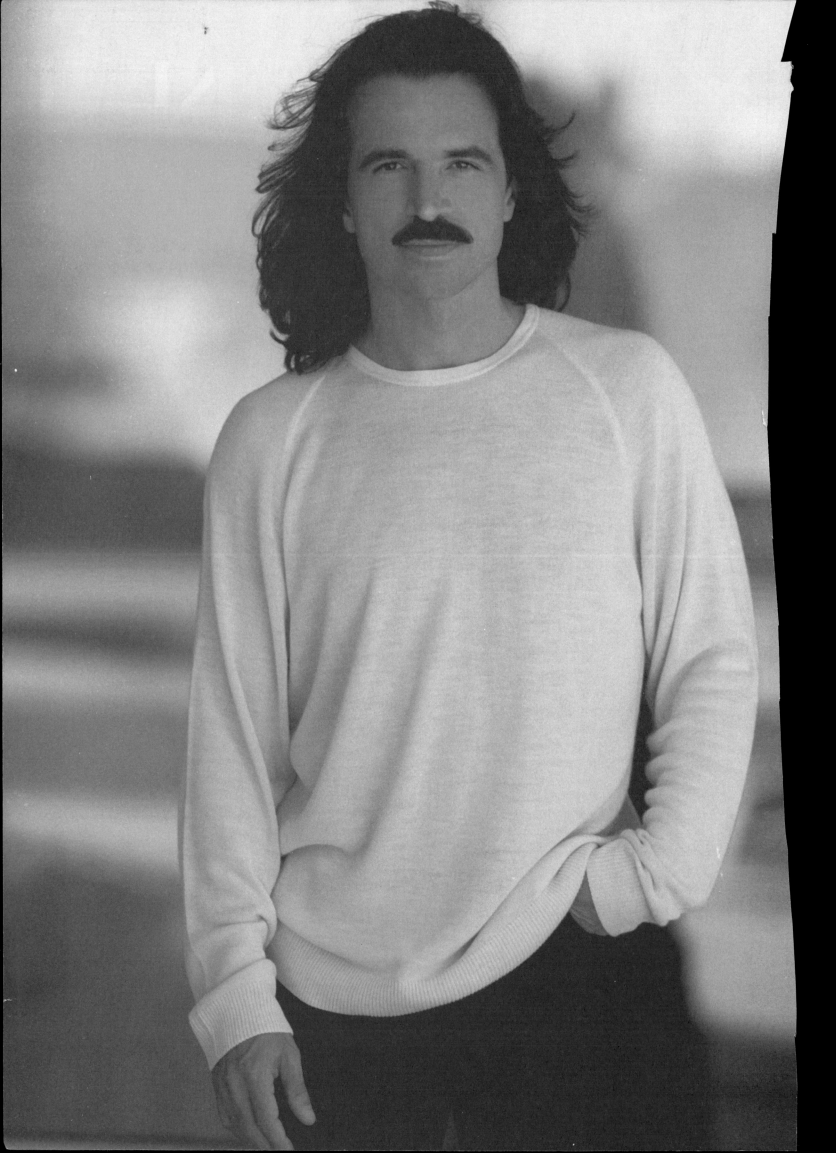

YANNI

SELECTIONS FROM
"IF I COULD TELL YOU" AND "TRIBUTE"

CONTENTS

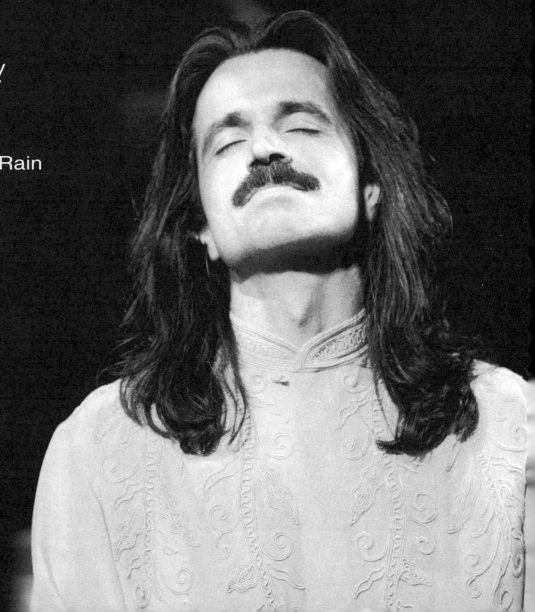

YANNI

BIOGRAPHY

He was born into a picturesque seaside village that no one ever gave thought to leaving and is now known in every corner of the globe. Yanni is, without a doubt, a musical phenomenon, one of those rare artists whose music defies borders and boundaries – whose music speaks to people of all races, all nations. And there is more than ample evidence to support such statements.

How many artists have become the favored composer of every Olympic broadcast for the past decade? Sold-out New York's Radio City Music Hall for ten dates? Played in the shadow of the Taj Mahal, the Forbidden City and the Parthenon, toured all of China and more than twenty other nations? Had a TV special seen in 65 countries by half a billion people, was one of the top fundraising subjects for PBS, and released what became the #2 best-selling music video? Mounted the #1-ranked concert tour for the first half of 1998 and #2 for the entire year? There is but one answer.

Yanni has always charted a solitary and distinctive path. A champion swimmer and self-taught pianist with the gift of perfect pitch, he left the comforts of Kalamata, Greece, on the spectacular shore of the deep blue Mediterranean, and then began to fashion his own kind of American success story, later to become an international success story.

After graduating from the University of Minnesota with a B.A. in psychology, after trading the Grecian sunshine for frosty winters, he would seek a life in music, though he could not read a note and wrote wholly original works, that, then and now, defy categorizing. From the beginning, he operated with a simple creed: a faith in hard work and keeping an open mind.

If I Could Tell You, which was released on October 3, 2000, is Yanni's 12th album. It is another provocative offering and confirms that his musical explorations have hardly ceased. The album is a fascinating tapestry, at once symphonic and modern, spellbinding and surprising, familiar and new. There are captivating melodies, sounds of many worlds, a powerful romantic energy. In other words, it's the work of a man used to taking chances.

This is an artist who invested millions of dollars into his *Tribute* project before a single sound was recorded, whose organization mounted a near biblical effort with the regional government of Uttar Pradesh to improve roads and build two bridges in order that the flood plains surrounding the Taj Mahal could be transformed for three historic concerts beneath one of the world's great wonders. A man who could have lost it all when an 11th-hour challenge was heard, but ultimately rejected, by India's Supreme Court.

The recording of the *Tribute* album would then proceed to China, where Yanni would become the first major Western artist to tour the country and then the first to stage concerts at another of the world's great architectural achievements, the Forbidden City. Once again, the concerts were beamed live. Between India and China, Yanni had played to a collective audience of 250 million people.

Tribute followed an earlier personal triumph when Yanni returned to his Greek homeland and recorded an album at the 2,000-year-old Herod Atticus Theatre in Athens. The result, the 1994 album *Yanni: Live at the Acropolis*, would be a sensation. It has continuously remained on the charts since its 1994 release, sold more than seven million copies worldwide, earned more than 35 platinum and gold albums, and rose to become the #2 best-selling music video of all time.

Yanni's first Grammy-nominated album was *Dare to Dream* (1992), which produced the vocal single, *Aria*, popularized in an award-winning British Airways commercial. His following album, *In My Time*, a gentler collection of piano-focused pieces, was also nominated for a Grammy.

"Music," Yanni says, "is an incredibly direct language. It bypasses language and logic, and speaks directly to your soul."

It is this notion that inspired the boy who began giving recitals before family members in a seaside village, and who has since been communicating on a global level that few of his peers can match.

ADAGIO IN C MINOR

Composed by YANNI

Slowly in 1, expressively

Steadily

THE FLAME WITHIN

Composed by YANNI

Moderately fast

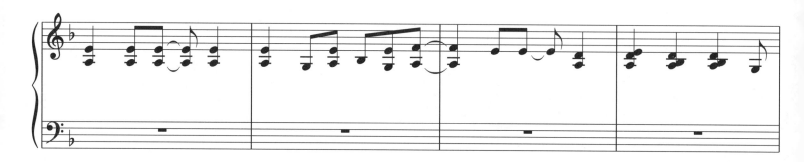

14

16

Repeat ad lib. and Fade

Optional Ending

HIGHLAND

Composed by YANNI

Moderately

To Coda ⊕

loco

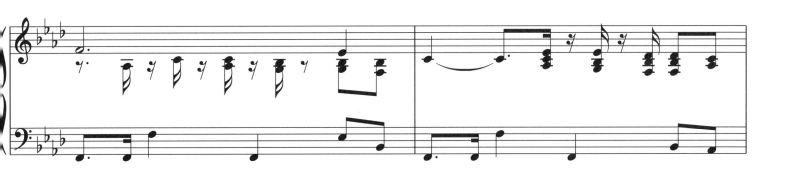

Repeat ad lib. and Fade | **Optional Ending**

IF I COULD TELL YOU

Composed by YANNI

D.S. al Coda

35

36

Repeat and Fade

Optional Ending

IN YOUR EYES

Composed by YANNI

Very slowly, freely

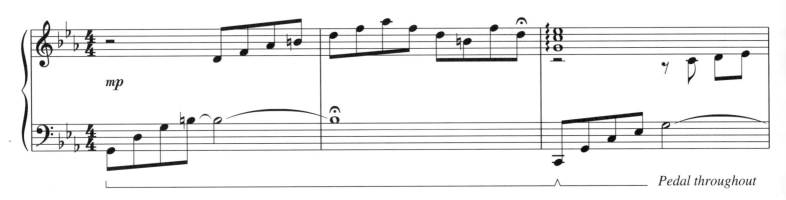

Pedal throughout

Moderately fast
(measure division: 3+2+2+2)

To Coda ⊕

NIGHTINGALE

Composed by YANNI

Very slowly, freely

Moderately fast

49

NOVEMBER SKY

Composed by YANNI

Moderately

Pedal throughout

59

Play 3 times

TRIBUTE

Composed by YANNI

Moderately slow

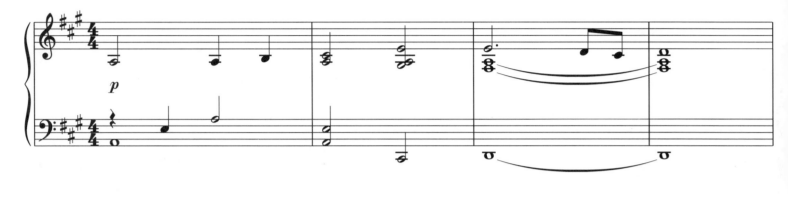

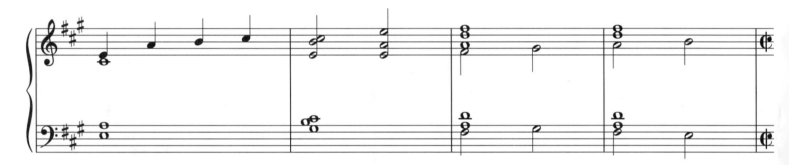

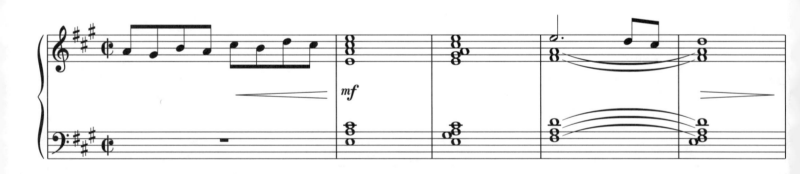

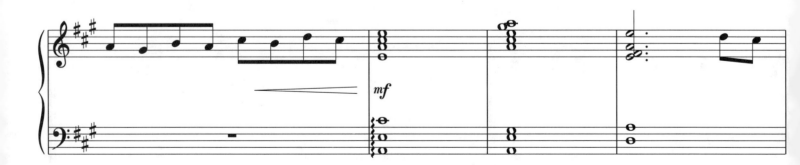

64

D.S. al Coda

CODA

68

71

WALTZ IN 7/8

Composed by YANNI

To Coda ⊕

cresc.

D.S. al Coda

CODA

A WALK IN THE RAIN

Composed by YANNI

Moderately slow, in 1

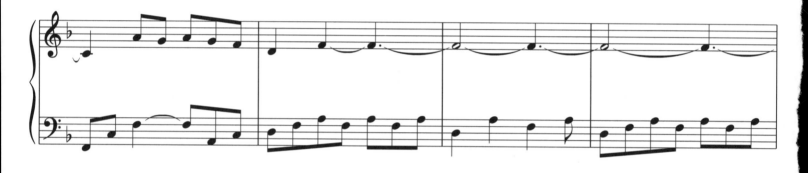

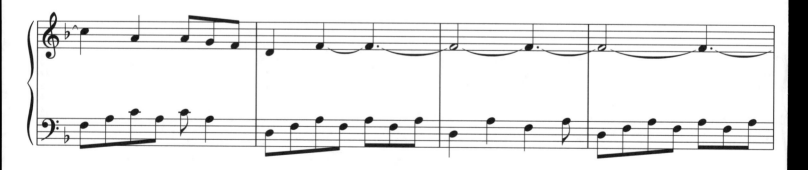

Repeat ad lib. and Fade

Optional Ending